CONTENT

SKETCHING STUFF ™

Doodlewash Books is an imprint of Doodlewash

ISBN 978-0-9600219-9-4 (Paperback)

DOODLEWASH is a registered trademark of Storywize, LLC. All Rights Reserved.

SKETCHING STUFF ™

Sketching Stuff™
sketchingstuff.com

CREATE LIKE A KID AGAIN!

Creativity is one of the most important tools we have in life. All jobs require some level of creative thought and, of course, parenting requires tons of creative thinking.

Thankfully, we were all born creative people! Like most behaviors that we already know how to do, we simply need to practice if we want to get better at doing them.

Together, we're going to go on a journey that will give you all of the tools you need to come up with your best and brightest ideas. No matter what job or creative hobby you want to improve, it all starts with Sketching Stuff.

By doodling, writing, drawing, and storytelling we'll create a sketchbook full of wonderful inventions. Amazing ideas await! It all starts with that next blank page.

> " It isn't just my heart that's young. My mind, my body, and my soul are all transported back to a time when hope made anything possible. I still believe in that magic. "

Charlie O.

2,000 DAYS OF SKETCHING STUFF!

Back in 2015, I found myself between jobs and in a bit of a creative slump. Then, my husband Philippe brought home some watercolor paints one weekend. I jumped in and played with them, and soon I was drawing again and coloring in the pages of a sketchbook. I then started a little blog called Doodlewash® and began posting not only my art practice for the day, but also stories of just about anything that came to mind. After 2,000 days of posting daily, I'd formed a habit that not only enhanced my creativity, but also taught me something far more valuable. A sketchbook was not simply a place to practice drawing, painting, and writing, it was a playground where my Inner Child and I could safely explore new thoughts. For me, "sketching" simply means the act of exploring any and all ideas. It's the first magic spark that leads to something amazing!

OVER 25 YEARS OF CREATIVE DIRECTION

When I was a kid, I wanted to be a million people when I grew up. In college, I was getting my art degree while earning money working as a real estate assistant, teaching tap and jazz dance, writing plays, designing sets and performing in musicals. After college, I continued on this course briefly, but soon committed to something adults call a "real job," meaning one that earns consistent income. I had a knack for ideas, so I soon became a Creative Director and have been some version of this job throughout my entire career.

Many people, including my entire family, don't really know what this job is, so I'm still uncertain if it fits the "real job" category. But it's been brilliant fun and has allowed me to work with hundreds of creators in all different fields. And best of all, I've learned a lot about creativity and what it takes to consistently come up with awesome ideas!

OVER 50 YEARS EXPLORING THE WORLD WITH MY INNER CHILD

Over the course of my life and career, one thing has stayed constant. I've always insisted on having fun and continued to see the world with the eyes of a child.

I love to look at life with fresh wonder and explore possibilities that initially seem quite impossible. I've had great success and massive failures along the way, but I've loved every moment.

I've learned that great ideas happen when we keep our minds and hearts open. That Inner Child is alive in all of us and when we truly listen, we can make magic happen every day!

ONE LITTLE BEAR

I still have my very first teddy bear. He's sitting on a shelf reminding me of when I was young enough to believe in the most magical thoughts. I had dreams bigger than any lifetime could accomplish. Yet, I had something more important. I had hope. I still do. Today, it's my hope to encourage others to connect with their own Inner Child and embrace their natural creativity!

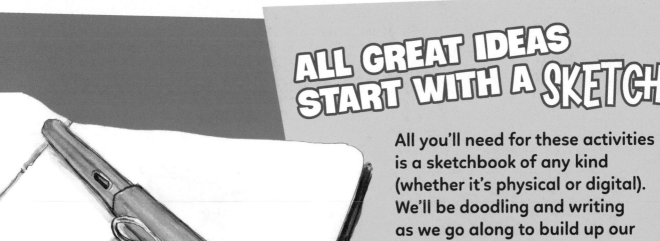

ALL GREAT IDEAS START WITH A SKETCH!

All you'll need for these activities is a sketchbook of any kind (whether it's physical or digital). We'll be doodling and writing as we go along to build up our creative powers. This will be an exciting and illuminating journey of ideas, and it all happens through Sketching Stuff!

WHAT KIND OF "SKETCHBOOK"?

DIGITAL

Though physical sketchbooks are great, I also love to sketch on an iPad® Pro with an Apple Pencil®. I really just love to doodle and everything becomes a "sketchbook" when I use it to scribble my images and thoughts. When it comes to writing, many love to journal in a physical journal, but I have trouble reading my own handwriting, so my laptop also becomes another "sketchbook" that I use to write stories and jot down ideas. My mind goes to a million places at once and it makes it much easier to catalogue those thoughts and find them later. So, I still prefer a laptop for writing, and it's how I made this book. Yep, digital tools are great for sketching stuff as well!

PHYSICAL

I adore sketching and doodling in traditional sketchbooks. I have stacks and stacks of sketchbooks that I've filled with my watercolor sketches. Seeing a stack of books always fills me with great pride. There's something unique and wonderful about the tangible nature of a physical book. So, I definitely think it's something everyone should try. Soon you'll have your own stack of little trophies filled with the wonderful ideas that you created!

&

HOW TO USE THIS BOOK!

This book contains over 60 fun exercises that are carefully selected to help you boost your natural creativity. But, as you'll quickly learn, it's a book that was created by and for that Inner Child inside all of us.

So, once you get to exercise #3, you can let that kid out to play and do whatever exercise peaks your interest in the moment. My hope is that you'll eventually complete them all, but creativity isn't a linear process. It's a messy and fun game of trying new things whenever the inspiration strikes.

Oh, and whenever you see this little image below, that means it's time to grab your sketchbook and create!

SKETCH STUFF!

Truly, this is a book about practicing creative play. There are so many rules in life, but there are no right or wrong answers here. So, let's begin!

Can't wait to Sketch Stuff? Let's try a warm-up! Doodle and/or write about 10 really creative things you've done in the past month.

RECONNECTING
WITH YOUR INNER CHILD

While they say that curiosity killed the cat, the reality is that curiosity has been scientifically proven to prolong our lives.

Life isn't about building to some future goal. It's really just a journey of discovery where we get to play and make lots of silly mistakes along the way!

But wait! Making mistakes isn't fun at all! Well, that all depends on how you make them and how you choose to react to them.

When we were very young, making a mistake was mostly just interesting. "Well, that didn't work like I wanted... I wonder what else I could try?" This mindset is exactly the one we want to cultivate when creating something new. Remember, if it hasn't been done before, then we don't really know what's truly possible. Developing a childlike sense of wonder is the first and most important step in our journey. But, it's not always quite as simple as it seems.

BUT I'M A GROWN-UP!

Learning isn't the same for me as it was back then!

It's true that as we get older, our minds tend to change when it comes to learning something new. We remember less and absorb less. And, we can now search online for the answer to practically everything.

If we want to learn about something, it's a matter of finding all of the steps and simply repeating them. But, when we follow that tried and true step-by-step process, we don't actually learn anything new. We simply learn how to do something in the exact same way that someone has already done it.

While this is still a great way to acquire knowledge, it's not a way to actually develop our creativity. For that, we need to leave the comfort of knowing and trade that in for a more ambiguous, and thrilling approach. It's not enough to imagine what it was like to have the wonder of a child. We need to truly feel that wonder again whenever we approach something new.

As grown-ups, our Adult Mind will often block ideas that seem a bit too far-fetched or seem too original. Why is that? First, let's look at a little science and psychology.

5 BRAIN MYTHS

AND WHAT NEUROSCIENCE TELLS US INSTEAD...

1 WE USE ONLY 10% OF OUR BRAINS

An oft-quoted misconception is that humans use only a small fraction of their brain potential. While it's interesting to consider some massive untapped brain reserve, there's no truth to this idea. In reality, we use nearly 100% of our brains over the course of an average day.

2 OUR BRAINS HAVE A PREFERRED LEARNING STYLE

While there have been claims that our brains prefer either a visual, aural, read/write, or kinesthetic learning style, it's not truly the case. It's simply more of a habit that formed. Recent studies have revealed that although people seem to know their perceived learning style and tend to use that more often, doing so doesn't actually help people learn more efficiently.

3 OUR BRAINS SEE THE WORLD AS IT REALLY IS

Information is constantly being processed by the brain as it enters through our sensory organs. We don't receive this information passively. Instead, we actively search for patterns to help us process. While this is very effective to quickly understand the world around us, it means we also tend to ignore patterns we weren't expecting.

4 OUR BRAIN IS HARD-WIRED

Our brains are often compared to electrical circuits, with fixed and predictable wiring. While it's true that our brains are organized in a certain way with particular areas specialized to handle particular tasks, our "circuitry" isn't completely fixed. Thanks to neuroplasticity, our brain has the ability to restructure or "rewire" itself when it recognizes a need for adaptation.

5

PEOPLE ARE RIGHT-BRAINED OR LEFT-BRAINED

Yes, it's true that certain kinds of tasks and thinking are often handled by one region of the brain versus another, but there's no such thing as a right-brained or left-brained person. Instead, we use our entire brain, even for tasks that typically would be associated with a different brain region. Creative thinking happens while using our whole brain in a very unique and highly efficient way!

3 BRAIN NETWORKS

EXECUTIVE CONTROL NETWORK
(Adult Mind)

This brain network is responsible for keeping focus and targeting your attention. It helps with decision-making and problem-solving for specific goals. I like to think of this as the "Adult Mind" that always seems to remind us of what's logical and reasonable.

SALIENCE NETWORK
(Sensory Switch)

This brain network monitors everything that happens in our internal stream of conciousness as well as all external stimulus. It acts as a sort of "Sensory Switch" to quickly alternate between the other two networks and help us choose which sensory information is most important when it comes to solving the problem at hand.

DEFAULT MODE NETWORK
(Inner Child)

This brain network is also called the Imagination Network as it's central to creative activities like brainstorming and daydreaming. I like to think of this network as the "Inner Child," always drifting off to fanciful places and dreaming up some of the most unexpected ideas. It's also responsible for our ability to empathize with the emotions of others.

YOUR BRAIN ON CREATIVITY

SCIENTISTS HYPOTHESIZE ALL 3 NETWORKS WORK TOGETHER!

DURING BURSTS OF INTENSE CREATIVITY, OUR SENSORY SWITCH TURNS ON TO ALLOW BOTH THE INNER CHILD AND ADULT MIND TO JOIN FORCES AND CREATE THE MOST INVENTIVE, YET PLAUSIBLE, SOLUTIONS!

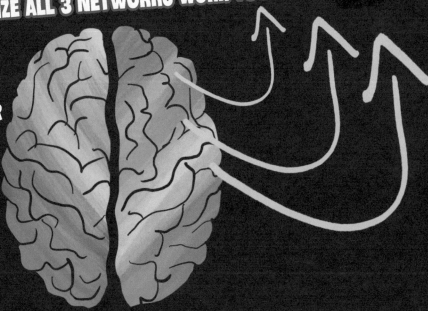

SENSORY SWITCH
(Salience Network)

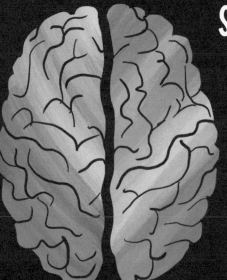

INNER CHILD
(Default Mode Network)

ADULT MIND
(Executive Control Network)

DIVERGENT THINKING

What would happen if you combined a typewriter and an octopus? Weird concept, right?

These are exactly the type of odd and wonderful thoughts that happen when we are in the act of divergent thinking. For this thinking mode, we throw caution to the wind and try to come up with as many ideas as possible. The wilder the better!

Yes, this is your "Inner Child" having a bit of fun. In order to make the most of this type of thinking, we need to reconnect with that sense of infinite wonder that we had as kids. It's what I like to refer to as creating a "what if?" list.

If we allow ourselves to dream a little, we quickly find that our ability to imagine is still quite endless. Just like when we were very little and didn't have all of the answers. Or, at least, didn't think we did.

As adults, we tend to think that our previous experiences have made us quite wise. In some cases, this is true, but much of the time, we're just comparing the present to the past as though they're the same thing. They're not. What worked last time we tried something similar to what we're contemplating today isn't guaranteed to be the best solution right now.

Coming up with lots of varied solutions allows us to see and make connections that we might have missed otherwise. It's a chance to open ourselves up to incredible possibilities. Yet, a ton of uncommon ideas alone isn't useful unless they can be made to work in reality.

Outside The Box!

LATERAL THINKING

CONVERGENT THINKING

You've likely heard the concept of "thinking outside the box." This refers to the act of "Lateral Thinking", a term coined by physician, psychologist and author Edward de Bono.

This thinking creates ideas that are wholly original, yet also seem perfectly plausible. Often, these are ideas that become obvious after they appear and make us say, "why didn't I think of that?" To create ideas like this, we need to be able to simultaneously look at problems with a bit of fanciful thinking combined with pure logic.

It's not a linear process of starting out with a zany idea and then judging its value. It's a practiced approach of moving effortlessly between the two other thinking modes and arriving at unique solutions. With it, we can move from known ideas to awesome and incredible new ideas!

This type of thinking involves looking for the "correct" answer to a problem. Yep, it's the "Adult Mind" again giving us well-worn advice. Though, we did use this thinking mode all of the time as kids in school when we took exams that tested our memory.

Rather than make an attempt to creatively solve something, it's sort of a multiple-choice approach to solution-making. This is, however, an extremely important part of the creative process. It's where we introduce logic, critical thinking, prior mistakes and known solutions.

3 ASPECTS OF HUMAN PSYCHE
FROM SIGMUND FREUD

SUPEREGO
(Adult Mind)

This is the angel that's often depicted in cartoons, whispering a sense of moral conciousness into our protagonist's ear. It's also that part of our psyche that is the most self-critical, reminding us of approaches and social standards that we learned from our parents and teachers. It's our well-meaning inner critic that, while useful, can sometimes get in our way.

EGO
(Mediator)

This is the decision-making component of our personality. It seeks harmony between external reality, the impulsive demands of the ID, and the moralistic judgement of the SUPEREGO. By mediating between these desires, the EGO seeks to achieve balance. It's how we determine our sense of self on this journey of life. And, through pride and positivity, we can even give our EGO a boost!

ID (Inner Child)

This is that little devil from cartoons, always encouraging our protagonist to act on pure impulse. It's that part of us that immediately responds to our basic urges, needs, and desires. When we're born, we're all ID and it's not until we grow up that we develop our SUPEREGO and EGO. But the ID never changes or goes away. It holds our most primitive, illogical, irrational, and primal thoughts, which we can use to create inventive ideas.

FINDING THE THE PERFECT BALANCE

So what do our brain networks, thinking modes, and our psyche have in common? They are all ways to look at how we balance our Inner Child and Adult Mind. And, this remarkable ability to seek and achieve that balance is what makes us naturally creative people!

In a nutshell, this is how we function, think, and feel. No matter what, we're always in the process of balancing our thinking. Understanding how our brains work let's us do that uniquely wonderful thing that humans can do. We can create change. We can rewire our brains to more rapidly come up with creative solutions.

> "We were all born creative, and our Inner Child is always there, ready to inspire us!"

We can change how we look at problems and develop more inventive ideas. And finally, we can affect our perception of the world and pursue those ideas with positive hope and confidence.

We were all born creative, and our Inner Child is always there, ready to inspire us! No matter what creative project we tackle, it all starts by Sketching Stuff.

Join me as we learn to achieve that perfect balance in how we function, think, and feel. It's time to be amazing as we develop awesome ideas and create like a kid again!

WHAT ELSE COULD THIS BE USED FOR?

One of the most popular tests of our creativity comes in a deceptively simple way. In research trials, paticipants are asked to come up with alternate uses for a simple everyday object. This can be done with any object at all, but we'll start with this fork. How many different ways might a fork be used, other than for eating food? As a hint, look at the form and let your mind wander a bit. Imagine you've never seen an object like this and are experiencing it for the first time, like when you were a very small child. What would you imagine this odd object might be used for?

1

SKETCH STUFF!

YOU HAVE 10 MINUTES!

Grab your sketchbook and a pen or pencil and start the clock (or use a timer on your phone). Then start scribbling down as many ideas as you can think of for alternate uses of a fork. Don't worry about what appears on the page. Just keep doodling ideas until your time is up!

RATE YOUR IDEAS!

This test was created by Ellis Paul Torrance, a psychologist known for his research in creativity. Torrance built on psychologist J.P. Guilford's earlier work, who is credited for distinguishing between convergent and divergent thinking. Early tests were mainly used to assess the level of divergent thinking in children, and were ranked on the four scales below. Yep, that Inner Child again ready to come out and play! Let's see how you did.

Ideally, you should have someone else look at your ideas and rank them according to the criteria (10 being the best), but you can also do it yourself (be as honest as possible).

FLUENCY
(How many ideas did you doodle?)

1 2 3 4 5 6 7 8 9 10
● ● ● ● ● ● ● ● ● ●

ORIGINALITY
(How novel are the uses?)

1 2 3 4 5 6 7 8 9 10
● ● ● ● ● ● ● ● ● ●

FLEXIBILITY
(How varied are the ideas?)

1 2 3 4 5 6 7 8 9 10
● ● ● ● ● ● ● ● ● ●

ELABORATION
(How detailed are the ideas?)

1 2 3 4 5 6 7 8 9 10
● ● ● ● ● ● ● ● ● ●

How did you do? Think you can do better? Try again!
Then try this with a different common object like a brick, shoe, or paperclip!

TELLING STORIES

Creating ideas is only the beginning. In order to share our ideas in a meaningful way, we need to be able to effectively communicate them.

Stories have been told by humans for thousands of years. Long before the invention of the printing press and books, we told oral stories to help us celebrate the present and connect with the past. We use stories to educate, entertain, and connect on an emotional level. As we improve our creativity, we can generate tons of ideas. Indeed, coming up with ideas gets easier and easier with practice.

Having lots of new ideas is only the start of the creative process. The next step is to effectively communicate those ideas in a way that makes others listen and care about them as well. And, as we make our ideas come to life, our ability to connect with others on an emotional level is key to our creative success.

Ultimately, a great idea is only as good as our ability to convey the concept in a tangible way that's immediately understandable, and emotionally relevant. For that to happen, we need to embrace the power of storytelling.

THE POWER OF STORYTELLING

There are many different definitions for "story" and many people first think of something purely fictional. Then, we might think of true stories as well, meaning something we might see in a documentary. I like to think of all great stories as "true" stories, because even if the characters are imaginary, a really good story always needs to feel "true" from an emotional standpoint.

By harnessing the power of storytelling, we can make the most incredible ideas feel true. According to Aristotle in his Poetics, the best endings to stories are both "surprising, yet inevitable." Our best ideas, in any form they manifest, are those that delight others, yet tell a story that feels plausible in an extremely satisfying and enjoyable way.

(Inner Child)
SURPRISING
Yet Inevitable
(Adult Mind)

LET'S MAKE A STORY!

A story can be simplified to mean something with a beginning, middle, and end. We've all experienced this in books, but it's the same for any piece of art or consumer product. We see something for the first time (beginning), we interact with it (middle), and we have a reaction (end). This could be something as cathartic as a character arc in a novel or as seemingly simple as causing someone to smile. In all cases, it's a journey that creates an emotional response. It's how good ideas become truly great. Grab your sketchbook, and draw and/or write the rest of this story!

Once upon a time, there was a little girl who could fly...

2 SKETCH STUFF!

RECAP
WHAT WE'VE LEARNED

Let's pause and review everything we've learned about creativity so far.

1 HOW WE FUNCTION

There are many myths about the brain, but we are indeed wired for creativity. We use our whole brain in a unique and wonderful way to create our most inventive solutions.

2 HOW WE THINK

Combining the power of divergent thinking simultaneously with the rationality of convergent thinking is the key to thinking outside the box. Lateral thinking provides our most creative, yet constructive ideas.

3 HOW WE FEEL

We may not actually have a little angel or little devil sitting on our shoulders telling us what to do, but we are always balancing our primal impulses with everything we've been taught to believe. How we balance these often competing impulses creates our sense of self. And we always have the power to give ourselves a positive EGO boost!

4 HOW WE COMMUNICATE

Storytelling isn't only something found in books. It's what humans have always used to effectively communicate ideas. When we look at everything we create as a story, we can begin to improve our ideas by taking people on a journey that's surprising, emotionally relevant, and perfectly plausible.

5 ULTIMATELY, THIS IS HOW WE CREATE

Whether it's our brain function, thinking approach, pysche, or communicating in story, our INNER CHILD and ADULT MIND are always there, working together to create amazing ideas!

READY TO POWER UP?!

6 THE CREATIVE SUPERPOWERS

These are the 6 creative superpowers we'll train and develop that will make your ideas fly to new heights!

1 Intuitive CURIOSITY

Developing a Childlike Sense of Wonder

2 Imaginative PLAYFULNESS

Creating Ideas Born From Pure Fun

3 Compassionate EMPATHY

Understanding Others through Shared Feelings & Experiences

4 Positive THINKING

Leading with Optimism, Harnessing Hope

5 Practical DREAMING

Generating Creative Solutions to Real-World Conundrums

6 Willful DARING

Being Bold Through Adventurous Courage

THAT LITTLE VOICE INSIDE

Sometimes, it's as simple as taking a moment to listen.

Before we begin more creative exercises, now would be a good moment to stop and do nothing at all. Wait! What! Let's get going!

Remember the Default Brain Network that I mentioned earlier? It's that natural resting state of our brains where we do something rather phenomonal. We daydream.

When I was little, I was often told that my "head was in the clouds." This wasn't necessarily meant as a compliment. It was someone telling me that I lacked focus. What they didn't realize was that I was totally focused on something else at the time. I was listening to a little voice inside.

This voice told me that I didn't have to follow all of the rules if breaking them meant creating something wonderful and new.

Today, that kid is still with me, and I credit him with all of my best ideas. And, I assure you that your Inner Child is still there as well.

Like all children, it just wants your attention and to feel truly heard. When you take time to listen, you'll find yourself thinking in completely new ways.

1 INTUITIVE CURIOSITY!

Developing a Childlike Sense of Wonder

CREATIVITY BEGINS BY GOING BACK TO THE START!

As we've learned, embracing your INNER CHILD is the key to superpowered creativity. Next, we'll discover ways to transport our minds back to when we were kids while we explore the world with fresh eyes to inspire new ideas!

When we were little, the world seemed full of more questions than answers. There were so many things we didn't know and it seemed like we would never figure it all out. In truth, a lifetime isn't enough time to learn everything there is to know. The world is full of mystery and wonders just waiting to be discovered. Yet, sometimes as adults, we tend to think we already have many things figured out.

When the Adult Mind is running the show...

While having a childlike sense of wonder seems easy to imagine, it's rather tough to achieve. Our Adult Mind often gets in the way by telling us what we already know. To look at something with fresh eyes and explore new possibilities, we have to turn off that Adult Mind for a moment so we can see the world much more clearly.

Letting your Inner Child out to play

When it comes to creativity, we need to suspend our disbelief for a moment and believe in wonders that only a child might find plausible. I often talk about letting my Inner Child out to play or letting him take control of my pen or brush while painting. My best and brightest ideas have always come from being in this state of endless wonder. While I'd love to say it's just a mental switch I turn on and off at will, the reality is, like most of the cooler bits in life, it takes quite a bit of practice.

Thankfully, there are lots of fun ways to practice this approach and the following are a set of some of my favorite exercises that will help you coax your own Inner Child to come out and play. Get ready to go back in time as we experience the world as if it's the very first time. Amazing ideas await! Join me as we master our very first creative superpower!

> Viewing the world too closely can often distort our view. It's very often best to take a few steps back, or indeed, climb up a tree, to see life more clearly.
>
> *Charlie O.*

MIXED-UP COMBO

Think of a common compound word. For example, a word like handshake. Then take one of the two words and change it to any random word. (like horseshake, or handmoon in our example) . Then take your new word and write and/or draw a story featuring that word.

3 SKETCH STUFF!

SUDDEN SPLASH!

For this exercise, we're going to start by splashing some watercolor onto a page in our sketchbook. Splash a bit of clean water on the paper, then dab in a few dots of different colors and let them go wherever they want. Once dry, take a look at what appeared there.

Like looking at cloud formations as a kid, what do you see? Grab a pen and scribble lines to make what you imagined appear!

4 SKETCH STUFF!

SCRIBBLE FUN!

Grab a pen and start scribbling on a page in your sketchbook, using big round gestures. Once you have a few lines drawn, stop and look closely at your scribbles. What can you see there? Grab something to color with, like crayons, and color in various shapes to reveal an image of some kind.

5 SKETCH STUFF!

MAKING NEW CONNECTIONS

When we view the world as a child might, we see things we weren't anticipating. One of the best moments in creative thinking is that moment when we see something unexpected. This something was there all of the time, but our brain makes totally new connections that allow us to see the world in a different light.

A random scribble becomes less random and begins to take shape as it transforms into something we recognize. And sometimes, two things that seem to have nothing in common come together in a way that just fits. These connections are central to creative thought.

Connecting thoughts and patterns in a new and unexplored way is the spark that has been responsible for every major breakthrough and invention we've seen, and for everything cool that comes next! This ability to connect seemingly random thoughts is something we see children do all of the time.

Yet, as adults, we often overlook these connections. Our brain wants to make "sense" of the world and tries to create familiar patterns. The exercises in this section will help you retrain your brain to look at the world in a new way.

This, in turn, will help you explore more random thoughts and wild possibilities. We are all capable of inventing something new and awesome, so let's make some new connections to help us do just that!

LOOK CLOSER

Look around your home and select a small, common, everyday object. Something you either use or look at nearly every single day. Pick it up and look at it very closely. Now, close your eyes and imagine it's something you've never seen before this moment. Open your eyes. Slowly turn the object around and look at it even more closely. Grab your sketchbook and write down 10 new features you can see that you hadn't noticed before. Then, without looking at it, draw the object next to those words!

6

SKETCH STUFF!

IMAGINARY TRAVEL JOURNAL

The world is full of places to visit, but sometimes we can't go on a trip. That doesn't mean we can't travel in our minds! For this exercise, we're going to go somewhere new. Think of a place you've always wanted to visit, whether real or imaginary. What's the most talked about feature of this place? How many inhabitants are there? What sights would be in the travel guide demanding that tourists can't miss them! Just close your eyes and imagine being in this place. Beyond the sights, what sounds do you hear? What smells are most prominent? See that road over there? Where does it lead? Take several minutes to truly explore this destination in your mind. Then, grab your sketchbook and write "Day One" at the top of a page. Below this, journal about your time there and everything you saw and experienced. Doodle something you saw on the page as you write as well.

What feels most important about this place? If you get stuck, just close your eyes and go back and visit. Let your imagination wander and you'll be surprised at what you find there!

7 SKETCH STUFF!

TAKE A JOYRIDE

It's time to ride in your car, jump on a bus, or hop on a train and go for a little trip. The only rule in this exercise is to go down a brand new road. No matter how many places we've been, even in our own town, there's always somewhere new to discover. Follow this new path and take a moment to simply look and see what appears. When you return home, write and/or draw everything you can remember about the ride. What did you see? How did it make you feel? Did you see anything you hadn't expected to see? Capture all of the memories you can in your sketchbook!

8 SKETCH STUFF!

BACK TO SCHOOL

It's the first day of school and you're nervous, and yet, just a little excited as well. That fluttering feeling in your stomach feels like it might be actual butterflies floating there. You've never been to school before and you've always wanted to be just like the big kids on your block. Today is the day!

Your teacher is very nice and welcomes you with a smile. Next, you're ushered to a little desk. "Good morning, class," the teacher says. You're ready to learn, but your mind is full of so many questions.

What question will you ask first? Grab your sketchbook and write down the question. Then write and/or doodle 5 different ways to answer it!

9 SKETCH STUFF!

FIRST-TIME CRAFT!

SOLVE A MYSTERY!

When we were little, mysteries weren't just stories told in books and movies. Many things that happened in the neighborhood had a bit of mystery to them. When you're looking at the world with fresh eyes, not everything is immediately explainable.

We're going in search of a brand new mystery to solve. Take a walk in your own neighborhood and look for something previously unnoticed. What if something weird or strange was involved? What can you imagine that might make the plot thicken?

When I was a kid, my mother was a master at all sorts of crafts. I learned how to sew and crochet when I was very young. I wasn't awesome at either, but it was so much fun to make something new that I didn't mind at all. We all have a craft that we've seen and admired and never tried ourselves. Now is our chance! Choose a brand new craft to learn. Follow a video or read a book and discover how to do something totally new. Just give it a go and have a lot of fun in the process. Then journal with words and images in your sketchbook to capture your experience!

Write and/or draw a short mystery story based on what you saw!

10 SKETCH STUFF!

11 SKETCH STUFF!

DISCOVER FUN FACTS!

Once, a very long time ago, I begged my mom to buy me an entire set of encyclopedias from a traveling door-to-door salesman. I still remember the crisp white pages filled with all sorts of wonderful information. For this exercise, you can use the Internet instead if you like and go in search of fun facts. Once you find the first new fact that you didn't know before, write and/or draw something to capture that fun fact in your sketchbook.

12 **SKETCH STUFF!**

INTUITIVE CURIOSITY

While it's always enjoyable to explore new ideas, sometimes as adults, it's tough to determine which new ideas are worth exploring. In the age of the Internet, it's easy to wander down a path of search results to discover something new.

Then, however, we usually just end up turning off our phones and going to bed. As kids, learning would usually turn into creating some sort of project. There was always more to find and more to discover than only the facts that were presented to us.

By listening to our Inner Child, we can renew that spirit of discovery we had as kids. Everything is worth exploring further and has the potential to lead us to something truly amazing.

Our Adult Mind will try to make the choice for us based on our experiences, but if we follow the intuition of that kid inside, we'll always find a more creative path to follow!

By CHARLIE O'SHIELDS / **33**

2 IMAGINATIVE PLAYFULNESS!

Creating Ideas Born From Pure Fun

WHEN WAS THE LAST TIME YOU TRULY LET YOURSELF PLAY?

The whole "adulting" thing can be really stressful. We might enjoy a bit of play with the children in our lives, but we're sort of overseeing the act. Next, with no children at all for an excuse, we're going to let our own imaginations out to play!

People often talk about "what they know now," and wish they could have provided their younger selves some of that insight. What I've learned is that this particular thinking is perfectly backward. My younger self already knew the most important thing in life — how to play and experience the fun that the world has to offer. So, I always try to tap into that sense of wonder and exploration.

Going beyond the possible

As adults, we tend to edit ideas too quickly. If something ludicrous pops to mind, it's easy to discount it immediately as just being silly or ridiculous. Yet, doing so limits us, and blocks us from imagining more inventive possibilities. When we think something is impossible, then we usually discard it and focus on the more probable solutions.

But what if we stopped doing that?

It's just time to play

While it's rather tough to get our Adult Mind to leave us alone entirely when we're working on actual projects, our sketchbooks give us full permission to play. Indeed, this sketchbook playground is like when we went to recess as a kid. We could play games we've always loved or make up our own games. We were limited only by our imaginations and never by the idea that imagining such things was a waste of time. But, going back in time is impossible, right? Nope! It's totally possible!

This next set of exercises will help us reconnect with our Inner Child by simply having a heck of a lot of fun! In the process, you'll discover new ways of thinking and, most likely, some fun new ideas that you'd like to pursue more in the future. But for now, let yourself do the unthinkable. BE that kid again and focus only on the imaginative playfulness that makes us each so creative!

I like the sound of someone's laughter. It's like listening to a person's soul. I think it's the sound of pure creativity at play, and it always inspires my imagination.

Charlie O.

DREAM A LITTLE DREAM

Close your eyes for a moment and imagine you've been shrunk down in size. You're now small enough to take a nap underneath a patch of mushrooms like this bunny. What do you see, smell, feel, and hear? What dreams might you have?

When we sleep, we can dream up the most incredible thoughts. Some people keep a dream journal to jot down those thoughts when they wake up. Often, those ideas can get a bit lost as we leave that space and explore our day. For this exercise, we're going to let our minds rest and let that Inner Child take us on a journey.

Draw and/or Write About What You Experience!

13 SKETCH STUFF!

BEDTIME STORIES

Remember when a parent would tell you a bedtime story just before you went to sleep? This bunny is super sleepy, so let's try creating a really quick one! Using just 10 words, let's tell a bedtime story.

Example: A bunny left home, traveled the world, and became legendary.

Write and Illustrate Your 10 Word Story!

14 SKETCH STUFF!

PLAYING WITH CONSTRAINTS

Activities like the ones on the previous page are more challenging than they seem. When we're sleeping, dreams are automatic and we're not usually a bunny. When we tell a story, we never have such a ridiculously low word limit imposed. Yet, when it comes to creative ideas, it's often the constraints that allow us to come up with the most clever solutions.

Indeed, when we begin to work out a new idea, it can sometimes feel overwhelming. This is often because we've not placed enough constraints on the project. With no guardrails or parameters, we inadvertently create a playground without a fence.

Conversely, sometimes we place the wrong constraints or too many on a project. So, beyond evaluating our ideas, we need to also evaluate the limitations we've placed on them as well.

JUMP FOR JOY!

Let's have some fun! Take one of the exercises on the previous page, change the constraints to whatever you like, and try again.

Don't want to sleep under mushrooms or be a bunny? Create a different dream scenario.

Want to create a 6 word story or a 6 page story? Choose whatever you like, then tell it your way!

15 SKETCH STUFF!

WORD PLAY!

Think of a common two word phrase. For example, I once thought about the phrase "flightless birds." I tried to imagine if those flightless birds could fly and ended up sketching a group of them riding on an airplane. Now take your phrase and think about it differently. What can you write and/or draw to illustrate it?

2 MINUTES

One of the greatest creative constraints is often time. A looming deadline when something has to happen quickly. Let's set a constraint of just two minutes. What could you create in such a short amount of time? Set a timer for just two minutes and start writing and/or doodling as many thoughts as you can that come to mind. Then try this same exercise 5 more times to see how your ideas evolve and grow!

16 SKETCH STUFF!

17 SKETCH STUFF!

MAKING A UNICORN

As adults, it's often tough, if not impossible, to remember a time when we actually believed in myths. Whether it was Santa Claus, the Tooth Fairy, or the Easter Bunny, we once thought the most wild and wonderful characters truly existed. When it comes to creating new and novel ideas, this is why kids often have the advantage. If you can imagine that anything is possible, then you can create the most amazing ideas. However, we watch movies and read books that often contain magical elements that we know aren't truly real. We suspend our disbelief. In this exercise we're going to do just that by creating a mythical creature. Write and/or draw something that describes a creature that has never been seen before by human eyes!

18 SKETCH STUFF!

10 CIRCLES CHALLENGE

Circles are like little planets of possibility!

Sometimes the best exercise for our creative brains simply comes from idle doodling. We've all doodled on a piece of paper or the edges of a handout, without thinking too terribly much about what appeared there. Sometimes it's just a squiggle, and at other times, it's something more representational. The trick that makes this type of doodling so fun is that we are barely aware that we are even doing it. And best of all, we have no preconceived expectations or monumental goal of trying to create a specific something or other. The lines that we make are the purest example of our own personal style. So, let's explore those lovely marks right now!

In this exercise, use a spread of your sketchbook and recreate the same pattern of circles that you see above (with 5 on each page). Use a large coin or the bottom of a glass to trace some circles on the pages as shown. Then just let your mind wander and start doodling to see what appears there!

Doodle in each of the circles, and feel free to draw outside the lines!

19 SKETCH STUFF!

THOSE FIRST FEW WORDS!

When we were little, making up stories was simply one of our play behaviors. We would dream up imaginary scenarios and, very often, craft complex plots filled with adventure and fun! Yep, we were all born with the gift of storytelling. So, let's put our natural talents to use and create a brand new story. For this exercise, we're going to create several suggestions of a story rather than writing the entire thing.

Use the model. "Once upon a time, there lived a [MAIN CHARACTER] who wanted to [GOAL], but had to overcome [OBSTACLE]. Try to write at least 20 different ideas. Then write a couple pages in your sketchbook, telling more of your favorite story!

20 **SKETCH STUFF!**

INSTANT FLASH!

Have you ever wondered how some people seem to always come up with awesomely creative ideas? They must just be more creative or more talented, right? Nope! Not at all! The secret is that they developed a practiced habit of quickly coming up with tons of ideas and simply pick the best one. Let's try it! Write down the first 40 ideas that pop to mind on what you could invent if you combined two common household objects and created something new!

Don't worry if the ideas would actually work or not in real life.

21 **SKETCH STUFF!**

LOSE YOUR MARBLES!

Sometimes the best way to break out of our usual habits and play without limits is to get really ridiculous. Like, imagine you're from another planet. Write down 10 completely made-up, silly words (check the Internet to be sure they don't already exist). Once you have them, write and/ or draw something that describes what each one means.

22 SKETCH STUFF!

IMAGINATIVE PLAYFULNESS

While the concept of being more imaginative is easy to consider, it's often harder to do as adults. We assume that the way kids play and think is something that only works for them. Once we've grown up a bit, we know what's real and what isn't and we sometimes think of being silly as something "childish." Yet, if we try to adopt a more childlike way of thinking, our ideas get instantly better. They are richer and more imaginative and much more surprising. Sometimes, we can even surprise ourselves with ideas that seem to come out of nowhere.

But, in order to get to those ideas, we first need to give ourselves permission to play without limits. We need to run through that playground screaming our fool heads off as we chase a unicorn around. Yeah, that's totally bizarre, right? Well, we wouldn't say that if we saw a child doing it. And, if doing that as an adult feels like you might invite a lot of uncomfortable looks from others, you're probably correct. We've been told over and over again how grownups are meant to behave.

But, you don't have to act like a child in public, when you can simply think those silly, childlike thoughts in private and capture them in a sketchbook. What happens next is really the most surprising thing of all. A wondrous notion that would never have come from your Adult Mind jumps forward and even that adult has to agree that it's actually a pretty awesome idea.

We never surprise ourselves by doing what always feels comfortable. When we move just beyond that "comfort zone" and do something unusual, the most novel thoughts pop to mind. Now that you know what they could become, my hope is that you make a habit of collecting these bits of thinking. Half-baked ideas are often the most powerful tools for creativity!

3 COMPASSIONATE EMPATHY!

Understanding Others through Shared Feelings & Experiences

EVEN THE MOST CREATIVE IDEAS COULD USE SOME LOVE!

When it comes to creativity, we can often get caught up in what's brand new. The most powerful ideas, however, always contain an element that feels rather timeless. Being able to truly understand and convey emotions is the next superpower we'll explore.

Do you ever find yourself crying while watching a sad commercial on television? Or, have you seen something bad happen to someone and it actually felt like you were in pain as well? Do you feel happy when you see someone else smiling? Sometimes, this is just a form of sympathy, but other times, it's something much more compelling.

The power of empathy

Empathy is the amazing ability to not simply understand another person's feelings, but to actually feel what another is feeling as if you were them. While it's easier to imagine when someone is very much like you, this gets more challenging with a person who is nothing like you at all. This is why it's often tough to discuss those polarizing topics like religion and politics. Yet, it's only when we can suspend our disbelief and truly feel another's story that we can create

something that has a high emotional appeal. Why is this important? Well, we humans have a habit of making decisions that aren't always rational. We might look for reviews on a new product, only after deciding we just had to have it. Learning to tap into this primal, visceral response in people can take a good idea and make it amazing!

Meaningfully significant

Sometimes ideas are just fun, cool, or unusual. We love to enjoy those ideas, but we tend to forget them as soon as we're done with the experience. Yet, some ideas are so much more. We see a piece of art, read a book, or watch something on television and come away from the experience with a lasting "something." It might be joy or sadness, but it's so real that we feel affected in a way that's forever memorable.

Next, we're going to practice a new superpower that allows us to connect with people on an emotional level to elevate our ideas to new heights!

> Technique is important for relaying information, but in the end, it's only our hearts that can truly express ideas.
>
> *Charlie O.*

IT TAKES TWO...

FROM THE HEART!

For this exercise, you'll need to partner up with someone. Think of someone you know who seems to have very opposite tastes who will play along with you. Ask them to make a list of their 10 favorite things to do for pure recreation and fun. Using this list, imagine you were them, and journal about why you love these things. There may be something on the list that you don't even like, but imagine why they might love it and write your thoughts from their perspective. Then, ask them to write about why they love each of the things on their list, and compare notes!

Often when we make a wish, it can be for something material. Perhaps we want to get that new job or to win the lottery. Those are wonderful events indeed, but they don't always come with a promise of happiness. For truly great moments, we need to wish with our hearts. Close your eyes and take a deep, cleansing breath, and say, "I wish..." without filling in the blank with words. Grab your sketchbook and start doodling, repeating "I wish..." out loud. Then describe in words what you see from the doodles that appeared on the page.

23 SKETCH STUFF!

24 SKETCH STUFF!

UNDERSTANDING HUMAN DESIRES & NEEDS

ONLY LOVE

The most memorable ideas in the world are the ones that touch our hearts. While some ideas might seem interesting, they move to a new level when we manage to create an emotional connection. This can be done with words, images, sound, touch, or a mixture of all of these. Anything that evokes our senses in some way will create a stronger feeling.

Often we can't articulate why something makes us feel a certain way or why we feel we need something. Though our brains are remarkably efficient, it's our hearts that make many of our decisions. It's that primal urge that draws us in and captivates us. Truly creative ideas find a way to do this by addressing the desires and needs of the audience simultaneously. For example, I might need a new appliance for the kitchen, but I want that particular one because of the way it looks and the way it makes me feel. Perhaps it's a bit of nostalgia that reminds me of my childhood or a time before when life seemed simpler. It's why one product, book, or piece of art sells quickly and another sits waiting.

As human beings we often think we know what others are feeling. But often, we're projecting our own feelings and worldview on others instead. Yet, there are universal feelings that we can all relate to, and it's those that we can use to connect with people on a much deeper level.

Much of our life involves a myriad of emotions. We can feel stress, pain, and sadness or feel joy and happiness. Yet, nothing compels us quite like love. It's not actually an emotion itself, but something that causes many emotions. And our brains need it to thrive and survive. For this exercise, write down 20 things you love most. Then cross out 10 of them, and then 5 more to end up with the 5 things you love most. Write and/or draw something that illustrates one of the most important things to you on that list.

25 SKETCH STUFF!

ALL THE FEELING

What are you feeling in this very moment? How about five hours ago? That second one is a bit tougher.

We tend to focus on feelings as they strike and not as a collected group of emotions. For a full day, write the time and journal about how you're feeling each waking hour. Circle the most positive feelings. Then draw and/or write about what was happening at that time.

27 SKETCH STUFF!

SOMEONE TO LOOK UP TO

As kids, there was always someone we looked up to in life. Not in the literal sense, though this was often true as well, but with a sense of admiration. Maybe our parents, teachers or someone famous that we wanted to be like when we grew up. Think of someone you admired most as a child and then think of someone whom you admire most today. Then write and/or draw something that illustrates a conversation between your childhood idol and your current one (if they're the same person, that's fine, they're older now).

THE MOOD RING

Though some folks can be described as "moody," we humans cycle through tons of moods in a given day. When I was a kid, mood rings were super popular, as they changed color to tell you what you were feeling in the moment. For this exercise, doodle the first thing that comes to mind using your favorite color. Then choose your least favorite and do the same. What appeared there?

26 SKETCH STUFF!

28 SKETCH STUFF!

CREATE A
LOVE STORY

We've all experienced love in some way, whether it's of a romantic nature or the love of a family member or close friend. When we love someone deeply, we form a very tight bond. With a parent, this story begins at birth. But with friends and romantic partners, this story starts much later.

For this exercise, we'll be choosing a friend or romantic love interest and creating a story of some kind. But, instead of an actual friend or lover, we'll be creating a fictional one based on those feelings.

First, write and/or draw the experience of your first most memorable encounter of this type (it might be a first love or early friend and not someone in your life today).

Be descriptive and try to relive that moment in detail. Think beyond the feelings and try to recall it with all of your senses. Don't worry about writing or drawing something perfect, simply something that helps you remember as much as possible. Feel free to take your time on this one and even add thoughts to your sketchbook over a couple of days.

Now, we're going to begin creating our story. Invent two characters that are completely different. Write and/or draw something that describes these two new characters in detail.

Next, create a scenario that is nothing like what you experienced as to how and where they met. Perhaps, it's a change to a more exotic location, different careers, etc.

Lastly, tell the story of these two new characters in words and/or doodles. Describe how they meet and any challenges they face. Try to really focus on describing all of the feelings and emotions that they feel. Be as descriptive as you can.

29 SKETCH STUFF!

SOMEONE ELSE'S SHOES

Think about something you've been struggling with lately. Perhaps a problem at work or home, or a creative project that doesn't seem to be coming together like you hoped. Next, think of someone who is your direct opposite, either in your life or someone famous. In your mind, pose your problem to them.

Write and/or doodle about what solutions they would offer to you. What would this person do in your situation?

30 **SKETCH STUFF!**

GRANDMOTHER'S QUILT...

When I was a kid, my grandmother made me this quilt from old bits of fabric. She's no longer with us, but I still have this quilt and it's one of my most treasured possessions. It's her hand in every stitch to be sure, but the fabric came from clothes that my mother used to wear as a child. This patchwork of memories was lovingly put together to create a blanket that not only provides physical warmth, but also manages to warm my heart.

Write down the top 10 most wonderful memories that you've had in life, from childhood through adulthood. Then, grab some old magazines and cut out images to create a collage in your sketchbook that illustrates all of those memories!

31 **SKETCH STUFF!**

THEIR FAVORITE FLOWER

For this exercise, ask a few people you don't know very intimately to reveal their favorite flower, and why it's their favorite. Then pick the flower you like least. Find some fun facts online and write those next to a doodle of the flower in your sketchbook. Then describe what you love about it.

32 SKETCH STUFF!

COMPASSIONATE EMPATHY

While getting into the minds of others can be tough, the most challenging thing to do is get inside their hearts. We tend to gravitate toward others who share similar interests and views on life. It's easiest to understand someone when they're very much like you. Yet, it's far more difficult to gain that same understanding of someone quite different than you.

Though we've all had moments in our lives where we've connected with the emotions of people in surprising ways, it's not always a habit. Instead, we are more often in a habit of turning inward and viewing the world through our own personal emotions. Many times, we think this must be what everyone feels, right? Maybe, but it's often worth taking the time to find out. I've always tried to make a point in my life to connect and listen to people who share opposing views.

I'm not interested in changing their minds, but simply interested in listening to their hearts. It's difficult and takes time and practice. What might normally evoke an argument is instead turned into a learning experience. I try to live by the rule that "everyone has something to teach me."

So, as we build amazing ideas and create the newest, coolest concepts we can dream up, it's important to imagine how others might feel. Is there something we can do to our idea that makes it more universal? Is there a way to improve it by adding a bit more heart? When we practice our Compassionate Empathy, we're not simply learning about others, we're finding out more about ourselves. And, if we can then apply that knowledge as we create, we can make ideas that are more meaningful, and resonate with more people in the ways that matter most.

4 POSITIVE THINKING!

Leading with Optimism, Harnessing Hope

LEARN TO IMAGINE THAT ANYTHING IS POSSIBLE!

Our Adult Mind thinks it is so wise, and it truly has absorbed a lot of information about the world. Sometimes, the focus is on what's failed before and is therefore impossible. But, our Inner Child has other ideas.

People have often told me that I'm an incurable optimist. I take great pride in this, as it's definitely a happier way to live than being pessimistic about life. Yet sometimes in saying this, people are saying that I'm not a realist. This is someone who simply accepts a situation for how it is and deals with it accordingly. I tend to imagine a better situation and then set about trying to create change. I know there are times when this doesn't work, but even the chance that I can make a better situation is worth the effort of at least attempting to do so.

I can't do this! I'm not that good at it!

One of the worst features of our Adult Mind is its ability to be overly critical of nearly everything new we attempt to try. If we're not immediately successful, then doubt creeps in and, in an effort to protect our Ego, tells us to move on to something else. Yet, there are no shortcuts to getting good at something. It always just takes practice. If we embrace our Inner Child instead, we can shut out that naysayer of a voice and focus on enjoying the experience. Our goal should never be "to improve," but simply to keep right on practicing. This takes away all of the pressure so we can focus and protect the joy that made us want to try something new and fun in the first place.

Remembering what it takes to feel good

Let's face it. When it comes to being an adult, we've built up a lot of walls around ourselves. We feel that we've mostly defined who we are and what we are capable of doing. We've grown up, after all, right? Not really. We just got older. At no point in our lives could we ever really know everything there is to learn. And when we live by maintaining a sense of childlike wonder, we can learn to always lead with optimism, and harness hope to make the impossible feel possible once more.

> When I approach something through the eyes of a child, it becomes far less vexing. What if life were just that simple? Understand what "good" feels like and go to that place whenever possible.

THAT FAVORITE SONG

Find and listen to a song that was your favorite when you were very young. Close your eyes and let the song take you back to that moment in time. Then, open your eyes and...

Write and/or Draw What You Experienced!

33 SKETCH STUFF!

When I was a kid my parents were in charge of playing music in the house. I grew to love those songs of the singer/songwriters of the 70's that they enjoyed and music has always been inspiring to me. My favorite song has often changed over the years, based on what was happening in my life at the time.

BLUE SKY THINKING

We've all heard the phrase, "the sky's the limit" But, what if there were no limits? Imagine for just a moment that you have magical powers and can make anything at all appear. Not something that exists already, but something you wish would exist. Got it in mind? Now how could you use your powers to make it even better?

Write and/or Draw What You Imagine!

34 SKETCH STUFF!

SEEING NEW POSSIBILITIES

While positive thinking is typically seen as the same as being optimistic, I feel it's so much more than that. To me, it's about opening both our minds and our hearts at the same time and letting new possibilities pour in.

Many of the good ideas that we miss along the way are ideas that we immediately discount as being unusable. This is based on years of living a life that always includes a few failures along the way. In reality, no two ideas are ever truly alike. There are always nuances that make them different.

Our Adult Mind desperately tries to form patterns and will immediately declare this version of the idea as identical to the last. At your job, you might have experienced your idea being shot down with the phrase, "we've already tried that before!" Before abandoning those ideas, we should always try to look at them with fresh eyes to learn and understand how, this time, it just might work!

As a creative professional and artist, my entire career is based on astute observation of the world around me. My eyes are important, but they tell only a piece of the story. Choose an object and study it very closely.

Look at every little detail that you can see and capture it in your mind. Now hide the object and close your eyes. Imagine it in your mind. Open your eyes and write about and/or draw what you remember and capture each detail.

35 SKETCH STUFF!

SHAKE IT OFF!

As a kid I was considered a big nerd and I was a bit chubby. This meant that I was also an easy target for bullies and people who wanted to make fun of me. Those types of people never really go away and show up in different forms in adulthood. Some people can just be big jerks!

Think of five insults you've received in life. Maybe even something negative you've said about yourself. Write down those five in your sketchbook. Then write and/or draw something positive about each one. Find a way to turn the negative into something positive and flip that insult into something worthy of pride.

36 **SKETCH STUFF!**

ON SECOND THOUGHT...

For this exercise, you'll first need to find something new to do. Find a place that you've never visited before and go for a visit! Then draw and/or write about your first impression of that experience in your sketchbook.

After that, return to that place and experience it again. When you return, repeat the exercise in your sketchbook. Did you discover anything new? Did your feelings change about what you experienced the first time? Make a note of the differences.

37 **SKETCH STUFF!**

MAYBE THIS TIME...

Remember that time you had an idea to do something and it failed miserably? No? Then, you've had quite a gifted life. For the rest of us, we have quite a few of those little failures that we've experienced along the way.

Think about an idea you had for something that you felt didn't turn out like you had hoped. Something like a new craft project, a written story, a cooking experiment, or an art piece. The bigger the perceived fail the better! Got a real clunker in mind? Great! Let's try to make it again!

Using the same elements as before, recreate the experience. Try to keep the basic idea the same, but feel free to make any little tweaks you like along the way.

Do you consider this time a success or a failure? Write and/or doodle your thoughts in your sketchbook.

38 SKETCH STUFF!

WEATHERING THE STORM

We all have our favorite types of weather and our least favorite. Some prefer rainy days and others prefer sun. Think about your least favorite type of weather. Then, write and/or draw something that describes only the positive and wonderful features of a day like that.

39 SKETCH STUFF!

A LETTER FROM MY YOUNGER SELF

Let's check in with our Inner Child and find out what advice is on offer. For this exercise, imagine you're a little kid again. Think back to a time when you were really young and what you thought you wanted to be when you grew up. Perhaps it's something totally different or maybe it's the same profession you have now. Think of all the dreams that kid had and everything that was imagined for the future. What did that child want to see happen? What were the biggest goals? What was the most important?

Write a letter as your younger self to your older self (and feel free to doodle in the margins!)

40 SKETCH STUFF!

BRAND NEW DAY!

Have you ever thought, "well, there's always tomorrow." This usually happens after a particularly bad day. Think about a real bummer of a day and relive it in your mind. Think about everything that went wrong or made you feel badly. Now, let's flip that bad day around. Write and/or draw a story of that day where each of the events that you wish would have happened actually do. Invent any wild scenario you like, as this is your brand new day!

41 SKETCH STUFF!

20 REASONS WHY I'M SO AMAZING!

I was looking in the mirror soon after I turned 50 and thought, "Wow, I look old. I used to be so much cuter than this." I actually spent the day feeling a bit bummed out. It occurs to me now that I was simply looking at myself in the wrong way. Instead of frightening faults, I should have been looking for fabulous features. Think about your own physical features and personality. Write and/or draw the 20 reasons why you're so darn amazing! (This time, it's okay to be a bit boastful!)

42 SKETCH STUFF!

POSITIVE THINKING

As we've seen, thinking positively is not blind optimism, but a real and powerful way to boost our natural creativity. When we imagine bigger and better possibilities, they will manifest as bolder and brighter ideas. It doesn't matter if something has been done before and failed. It doesn't matter if something seems too impossible to ever succeed. What matters is that we always try, and then try again, and again, and again.

Eventually, something wonderful always happens. Each time that Adult Mind tells us that we're not doing something well or that we're failing, we don't have to accept that. We can simply access our Inner Child and turn off that bit of our brain for just a moment. Maybe, it's wacky. Maybe, it won't work. But, we'll never know unless we try. There's nothing sadder than a dream that isn't allowed a chance to grow.

By adopting a positive outlook, with even just a sprinkle of hope, we can make the most incredible dreams come true.

5 PRACTICAL DREAMING!

Generating Creative Solutions to Real-World Conundrums

DREAM BIG DREAMS THAT BECOME A REALITY!

Our Inner Child is full of amazing ideas and knows how to dream big! Not every dream makes a lot of sense and the Adult Mind jumps in with practicality. When we learn to create with both opposing forces, we can make bigger ideas that really work!

As a kid, I would lie awake in bed at night and imagine all of the amazing projects I would try next. I would write a story or make the most amazing contraption to send marbles swirling around. The latter was just silly fun, as what on earth would be the purpose of that? I didn't really worry about the practicality of my dreams, I just wanted to pursue them to see what would happen next. It was super fun, and I always learned a lot in the process.

Dreams are great, but this is real life

As I grew up, I continued to dream of new ideas to try. And as a creative professional, I had to come up with brand new ideas every day. This time, however, they had to happen in real life. Unlike when I was a child, I now had others who would tell me my dream wouldn't work. That it wasn't possible. I've learned that some ideas were a bit too outrageous. But, more often, I learned that with a little more imagination, I could make even the wildest ideas into something that had real-world practicality. Finding that perfect mix requires a delicate dance between the two usual suspects.

Letting the child dream

Our Inner Child dreams big, and we have to let that happen a bit before allowing the Adult Mind to judge those ideas. Too often, we can begin to judge ideas before they have a chance to shine. It can seem easy to notice the flaws in something, but sometimes they aren't really flaws at all.

They are opportunities. A chance to explore the edges of possibility and come up with something truly new and novel. When we want to create a fresh approach, we need to suspend our disbelief a bit longer than we normally would. Only once we've had a chance to fully explore ideas should we begin to judge them on their merit. We'll need to be practical at some point, but that should never limit our ability to dream bigger dreams.

> **Possibilities are limited only by our dreams and imagination. Life has always been a dance between logic and dreams, and I love each step along the way.**
>
> *Charlie O.*

DREAM, THINK, INVENT!

Let's invent a smart new product! Dream about something impossible that you wish were actually possible.

Think of 10 absurd ways this "could" be made possible. Pick your favorite. Name and describe your product with words and/or drawings.

43 SKETCH STUFF!

THAT MOVIE

IN YOUR MIND!

Let's make a movie! Okay, maybe not, but we can certainly create ideas for a movie. Dream up 5 movie concepts and write them down using this formula: When [SOMETHING INTERESTING HAPPENS], [OUR HERO] must [DO SOMETHING] to [STOP THE VILLAIN]. Choose your favorite movie concept and write and/or draw something that tells more of that story!

44 SKETCH STUFF!

STARGAZING!

A starry night sky always seems endlessly deep and full of possibilities. A constellation is a group of stars that form a perceived pattern. There are many famous examples like the Big Dipper, but those are patterns others have already determined. Take a long, fresh look at the stars. Find and name 10 new constellations that you can see!

45 SKETCH STUFF!

MAKING IDEAS COME TO LIFE

As a kid, I would dream the wildest dreams and, in my heart, I truly expected them all to come true. Growing older, I still love to dream up wildly improbable scenarios and my head is still filled with fanciful thoughts.

Can all of those dreams really come true? In a way, yes!

We have the amazing ability to take those sometimes random thoughts and pull them together into something that others will truly enjoy as well.

Throughout my career, I've found that being only practical leads to rather boring solutions. But when you add a healthy dose of dreaming to the mix, you can come up with magically inventive ideas that seem to have a life of their own.

While I adore that moment when an idea first pops into my mind, what I love most is the next thing that happens. Having an idea is only the start. The real challenge comes in taking that idea and presenting it in a way that others can understand. Beyond that, we need to get people to emotionally connect with the idea as well.

Practical Dreaming brings our Inner Child and Adult Mind together in concert to create ideas that are magical <u>and</u> meaningful. And, with a bit of practice, we can learn to cleverly play with dreams and use them to help us solve real-world problems.

That next great innovative thought is waiting to come to life. It's just a heartbeat away from that next really big dream!

WINDOW VIEW

Take a moment to sit by a window in your home and look outside. Do you notice how your eyes tend to take the scene in at a glance, and make everything seem perfectly familiar? Close your eyes and imagine the scene instead for a few minutes. Open your eyes, then write and/or draw what you saw.

46 SKETCH STUFF!

DREAM! DREAM! DREAM!

Do you remember what you dream at night? Does your mind tend to wander to other random thoughts during the day? Many times we aren't able to remember the dreams we have at night. As our brains switch to reality, those thoughts we were having rapidly disappear. Also, we can tend to forget what we were just daydreaming when we suddenly have to focus on something that's currently happening. These thoughts and ideas are pushed to the back of our minds and can get lost. As we learned earlier, these dream states occur when our brains are in Default Mode. This is the mode I refer to as the Inner Child and it's one of the most important modes for developing stronger creativity. So how do we capture our dreams before they disappear into the mist? For this exercise, we're going to use our sketchbook as a dream diary and capture all of the dreams we can as soon as possible after having them. For the next 5 days, write and/or doodle everything you can remember about a night dream as soon as you wake up as well as any daydreams that you have. What's the most common recurring theme? Write and/or draw something that illustrates the theme. Or, if a wonderful idea for a project appears, try to elaborate on that concept!

47 **SKETCH STUFF!**

THEY'RE ALL DUMB IDEAS!

Sometimes dreams don't make a lot of sense. In this exercise, we're going to actively try to come up with the worst, silliest, most ridiculous ideas we can! You've been tasked with dreaming up a brand new product. When you receive the creative brief, you immediately realize it's not much to go on. The company wants to create a new type of breakfast cereal and needs a catchy name and a character mascot to appear on the box. They haven't even yet figured out what the cereal will be! What the heck? Okay, grab your sketchbook and write and/or doodle 30 super wild and ridiculous ideas for a name, character mascot, and type of cereal. When you're done, look through the ideas and choose and elaborate on the ONE that's just zany enough to work!

48 SKETCH STUFF!

ANOTHER PLANET!

The universe is a vast place and much of it has yet to be explored. Beyond our own galaxy are trillions of other galaxies waiting to be discovered. Is there something like our idea of intelligent life out there? It's very likely, however, we might not be living during the time when we finally make contact. Instead, we can do what artists and writers have been doing for centuries. We can simply dream of what's out there. For this exercise, we're going to create our own planet! Whoa! That sounds wacky, right? Good!

That's always a promising first sign that something will be fun and awesome. In your sketchbook, draw a large circle and then color it however you like to create the look of your planet. Next, point to key features that you see and describe what's there. After that, take us on a journey there. Write and/or draw a story about a day in the life on your planet.

49 SKETCH STUFF!

CONTEMPLATING THE MOON

People often say that they can see a face on the moon's surface. This is our wonderful brain at work trying to create something recognizable using patterns to explain those dark splotches. These are called maria, Latin for "seas" as that's what early astronomers thought they were seeing. Neither is true. Those dark patches are instead remnants of ancient volcanic eruptions.

But knowing that shouldn't stop us from dreaming up something else. Examine the moon closely and let your mind wander. Write and/or draw 10 imaginative things that you see on the moon!

50 **SKETCH STUFF!**

REAL & IMAGINED!

Sometimes the most beautiful creatures in nature seem almost otherworldly. A peacock is gorgeous, yet also a rather strange invention when you think about it. There's a reason for each pattern, color, and appendage, but unless you study facts about this bird, it's not immediately clear. For this exercise, choose an exotic animal of some kind with intriguing features that you know nothing about. Then, doodle that creature in your sketchbook and draw lines outward from the most interesting features. Write your own fun facts, dreaming up what you imagine to be the function of each feature.

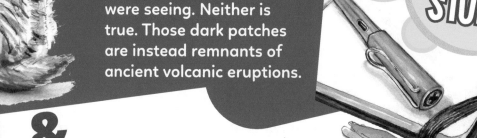

51 **SKETCH STUFF!**

FRESH SNOW!

As a kid, I loved waking up to a blanket of fresh snow on the ground. I couldn't wait to go outside and play and hopefully make a snowman or some other amazing creature. In my excitement, I didn't have a strict plan, I was just happy to make something new. Open your sketchbook to a blank page and imagine it as fresh snow. Immediately start doodling whatever images and words come to mind. Choose one thing from this page and write and/or draw something on the next page that expands on that idea!

52

SKETCH STUFF!

PRACTICAL DREAMING

Dreams are a powerful part of our creative process. Daydreaming tends to be considered problematic, by distracting us and causing us to lose focus. Yet, it's often the exact moment when we see ideas more clearly.

By letting our dreams form without trying to edit them, we give our minds time to consider all possibilities. Too often, our Adult Mind jumps in to make an assessment of that absurd thought we just had way too soon.

For creativity, we need to give our brains the time and space needed to dream properly. This requires letting our wildest thoughts form and reform before we attempt to shut them down entirely.

That's why it's great to capture dreams in your sketchbook before they disappear. Save all of those wondrous thoughts as you go, and make a habit of embracing them.

Then you can go ahead and let your Adult Mind take its moment to judge and sort them, searching for the more practical solutions. The more we dream and play with ideas, the more we end up with ideas worth keeping. And though having one's head in the clouds can seem unproductive, it often provides the best view.

Whether we're creating new ideas or trying to riddle out a solution to a vexing problem, our dreams can help guide us. By letting our Inner Child explore freely, we can then use our Adult Mind to add just a touch of practicality to the mix.

In this way, we can mold even the most outrageous and impossible dreams into a brilliant idea that will actually work in the real world. Always dream big and capture each spark of imagination you can along the way!

6 WILLFUL DARING!

Being Bold Through Adventurous Courage

TAKING RISKS HAS NEVER BEEN SO MUCH FUN!

It's time to master the final superpower and discover the hero inside. Yep, inside each of us is a courageous person who is just one great idea away from becoming legendary.

Being bold in our approach to creativity and the creation of new ideas is one of the most important skills needed to succeed. Did I say skill? Aren't some people just more naturally daring than others? Well, yes, many people seem to have courage in spades, but we all have the power to become bolder in our approach. Like every skill, it just takes a lot of practice.

And, in this case, it also takes learning to embrace mistakes as an important part of the learning process. In fact, we should go farther and celebrate mistakes along the way. If everything is going smoothly, it's usually safe to say we're on a dull and expected journey. When we step outside that comfort zone, there aren't many guarantees, but I guarantee you'll have a lot more fun with the right attitude. And those wildly creative ideas will come more easily.

Bravery vs. Courage

Bravery is an inherent trait that some people are lucky to possess. That means they experience no fear and instinctively jump to action, even in a dangerous situation. I've personally never been that cool. I get scared all of the time. Most of the time, it's a fear of screwing up and failing at something. Courage, however, is the ability to acknowledge a scary situation and still manage to act even though you're afraid. That's something that also just takes practice. In other words, we don't have to remove our fears in order to act, we just have to learn to embrace them and move forward anyway.

Practicing Courage

For our final superpower, we're going to practice being more courageous. And best of all, we're going to do so while having a ton of fun in the process. We'll face those silly fears with our Inner Child and practice our Willfull Daring in this last set of exercises.

> I had none of these silly fears as a child. No fear of falling, nor any fear of failing at something. I knew that I could simply try again, so I never really made a fuss about doing so.
>
> *Charlie O.*

FACE YOUR FEARS!

STACK 'EM HIGH!

Think about something that scares you more than anything else in the world. Perhaps it's something tangible or intangible, but whatever it might be, the thought leaves you a bit terrified. Have something in mind? Write down all of the reasons you can as to "why" this scares you. What is it that you're most afraid of? What reasons can you give for why this scares you? Write as many fears as you can and be as descriptive as possible. Then, draw something that illustrates what you fear most in your sketchbook. It can be a simple doodle or something more elaborate. Then turn the page and draw the same thing 5 more times.

Sometimes, when creating, we stop too soon. An idea feels good or safe and adding anything more would make the entire thing topple to the floor like a wooden block game. But, if it's all just a game, then why not have some fun? Write about and/or draw a simple idea for a product of some kind and then keep adding features to it. Add as many as you can, and be as silly as you like! Once you've created your contraption, remove ideas that you like the least by marking them out. Then sketch what remains on a fresh page.

53 SKETCH STUFF!

54 SKETCH STUFF!

COURAGEOUS EXPERIMENTING

The best thing about courage is that it exists because of fear, not in spite of it. You don't have to worry about actually being brave, you just have to keep experimenting, even when those fears start to creep in. Sounds easier said than done, doesn't it?

Well, if you go way back in time to when you were a small child, you'll remember doing lots of new activities. In fact, most of our childhood is spent discovering and learning something new each and every day.

I always loved learning, but I wasn't good at everything I tried. I was terrible in gym class, for example. We had to climb a thick piece of rope for a physical challenge once and I was terrified. My lanky arms were not strong enough to lift my chubby grade school body.

But, I was determined to try. So, I jumped at that rope and started to climb. Did it work? Not at all. I hung there like clean laundry just willing my arms to pull myself up.

It was something I just couldn't physically do. The gym teacher gave me something else to try, and I can't even remember what it was. I did it, as the teacher assumed I would, and I was proud again.

I learned that failing at one thing didn't make me a failure. It was just about experimenting with various approaches to learn what worked and what didn't for me personally.

I was still scared that I might not succeed, but I was more interested in finding out what happened next. I became more willful about jumping into new projects, as I simply dared to try.

JUST OUT OF REACH

One of the most challenging aspects of practicing a skill is knowing when it's okay to move to the next level. It's often hard to improve at something when we find our comfort zone. Think about a creative hobby you currently enjoy. What's the next thing you've told yourself you'll try when you're "good enough"? Now, do that very thing right now! Then journal about your experience.

55 SKETCH STUFF!

THE MUSHROOM FOREST

When it comes to creativity, we don't always know what lies ahead on our journey. It's a bit like a small child in a fantasy story who embarks on an adventure in a strange and unfamiliar place. In a story, turning back is never really an option, even when the main character is afraid. If that happened, the story would end before it even had a chance to begin.

The same thing happens to us when we're trying something new or working on a new creative project. If it's for work, someone is imposing a deadline and expectations so we're nudged forward no matter what. But, when it's a personal project, we often only have ourselves to urge us along. I have sketchbooks full of half-grown thoughts and bits of concepts that I abandoned. When I look back at them now, I see glimmers of merit in many of those ideas. Why didn't I continue down that path? What was it about that particular forest of thought that made me stand at the precipice without moving ahead?

Most of the time, I've found, it's not because the idea itself was a bad one. The notion just seemed too grand to tackle in that very moment. It's one of those notions that I call a "someday idea." And, we all have them. Those ideas, we haven't dared to start yet.

This book is one of mine. What's one of yours? Choose one of your "someday ideas" and revisit it now. Write and/or draw something that moves that project forward, even if it's just a couple of steps.

56 SKETCH STUFF!

WHEN PIGS FLY

Think of something truly impossible. Or, at least something that seems completely impossible. Then, truly imagine that it's actually happening or exists right now. Write about and/or draw something that illustrates this impossible thing and try to convince yourself that it's actually possible in the process.

58 SKETCH STUFF!

TOSSING THE BALL!

For this exercise, you'll need to partner up with someone else. We'll be using a technique that's the cornerstone of improvisational comedy called "Yes, and..." thinking. There's only one rule... you can't say "no" or judge what the other person comes up with, but must expand on what they say in any way you like! You can begin by talking about anything at all or even telling a story, then the next person says, "Yes, and..." to continue the story. After 10 exchanges, write and/or draw something inspired by the final spoken words.

57 SKETCH STUFF!

PLAY A NEW GAME!

Learning all of the rules and strategies for playing a brand new game can often seem daunting. It's much easier to simply jump in and play games we already know well. For this exercise, find a game (analog or digital) that you've never before played. After you've learned how to play it, play some more until you feel like you also understand how to play it better, more strategically. What would make the game even more fun?

Write about and/or draw something that would improve it.

59 SKETCH STUFF!

ANY WAY THE WIND BLOWS

Do you find yourself wishing you could just know what happens next? We all do this. Surprises are fun on birthdays, but the rest of the time, we just want to know what will happen. It can be unsettling when we don't know. Yet, as kids, not knowing was really all of the fun!

Write and/or draw the first thing that comes to mind. Then, keep adding to it, letting each idea take you to the next.

60 SKETCH STUFF!

FISH OUT OF WATER!

One of the most entertaining premises for a movie is a "fish out of water" scenario. A character who is leading one kind of life is suddenly thrust into completely unknown territory, and therefore, a new adventure! While this is fun to watch, when it happens to us in real life it's sometimes stressful and even scary.

For this exercise, write down all of the things that you believe are a comfort to you. In short, define and describe your "comfort zone." Then, imagine what you might do that's completely at odds with your comfort zone. Got it in mind? Now go and do it! Give it a try! Afterwards, write about and/or draw something that describes your experience in detail. What did you learn along the way?

61 SKETCH STUFF!

COLOR BOLDLY!

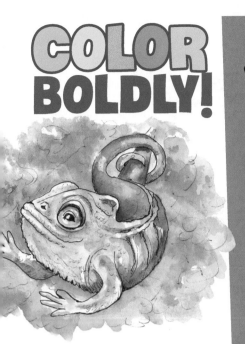

Often when I'm coloring something I've drawn, I start by choosing realistic colors. It feels more comfortable and well, safe. This is my Adult Mind telling me there's a "correct" way to do it. But, as a kid, I'd use whatever crayons I could grab and gleefully color with any colors that felt like the right ones in the moment. Doodle something in your sketchbook with a pen or pencil. From a pile of crayons, close your eyes and choose 3 colors. Using only those colors, color your doodle!

62

SKETCH STUFF!

WILLFUL DARING

This is the last of our creative superpowers, because it's arguably the most important. To get to more creative ideas, we have to be more bold in our approach.

We don't have to remove all of our fears, but we have to have the courage to move ahead in spite of them. It's not just being daring, it's doing so with a strong willfulness that you might only see coming from a very young child.

Before we let our Adult Mind try to discipline our wacky behavior, we have to let ourselves play and explore all possibilities. Like everything in life, it's just a matter of practice and forming a new habit.

Instead of falling into a habit of always staying in one's comfort zone, we need to form a new habit of always pushing the limits and stepping into new areas of thoughts and actions that are totally unknown.

Exercises like these are a wonderful way to practice this behavior. There are no expectations and no required outcome. It's just a way to play in a sandbox of thoughts and ideas.

Nothing truly new ever comes from playing it safe. Yet, as we get older we can feel a bit hard-wired with a need to always take the most comfortable and predictable path.

Your sketchbook is your own personal place to play and explore thoughts that might normally freak you out. If you think something you're writing or drawing is too weird to share, that's perfectly fine! In fact, it's probably preferred.

Chances are good that you've found something quite new that's definitely worth exploring. Today's weird thing can often blossom into something unexpected and amazing!

YOUR BRIGHTEST IDEAS!

Let your Inner Child out to play, dream and create!

We've learned how creativity works through how we function, think, feel, and tell stories. Along the way, we've also learned how to embrace our 6 amazing creative superpowers.

And, best of all, we've learned that we've had these abilities since we were kids. Our natural creativity is one of the most powerful tools in the world. Some people have chosen a career path where that creativity is required each and every day. Most people tap into that creativity more outside of work through various hobbies.

Yet, I contend that everything we do in life could be made more meaningful when we let our natural creativity sparkle all of the time. We can take anything in life that seems mediocre at first and elevate it to new heights! And, we can make both our professional lives and hobbies light up with exciting new possibilities.

It's just a matter of sketching them out and exploring each one with the wonder of a child. When we do that, our regular world becomes much more extraordinary and we begin to unlock our best and brightest ideas!

WHEN I GROW UP
I WILL ALWAYS BE CREATIVE!

No matter what the future brings, being creative is the one thing we can count on.

So, as you can see, growing up is a completely optional affair. We get older, and there's nothing to be done about that. But, we can still dream about something new that we'd like to try next. At any age, we can always change the very idea of what we want to be when we grow up.

Yet, my hope is that no matter what you want to achieve in life, you'll always do so with courage and glee. Whether you choose one path and follow it for a lifetime or choose to constantly run down new paths, as I have, there's only one way to truly succeed. We need to always find ways to harness our natural creativity along the way.

I know you're an amazing and creative person and I'm thrilled for your journey ahead. It won't always be perfect, but it will be perfectly amazing if you choose creativity at every turn. Let your Inner Child out to play and then play with all of your heart. The best part of any journey is always what's yet to come.

MORE FUN WAYS TO SKETCH STUFF!

While there are over 60 creative activities captured in this book, exercises like these are as infinite as ideas themselves. There's always something new to try and explore in the world. The key isn't really in any one particular activity, but in finding inspiring ways to practice looking at the world with fresh eyes.

When we can allow our minds to see the world as though it's the very first time, remarkable moments begin to happen. What truly inspires us as individuals will be quite different for each person. I've shared many fun exercises that I like to do, and I hope these will inspire you to invent your own fun approaches as well!

We can't learn how to be creative, because we were already born that way. It's not about learning so much as remembering back to when we were little kids and creativity was effortless. But, just for fun, here are a couple more approaches to help spark your imagination!

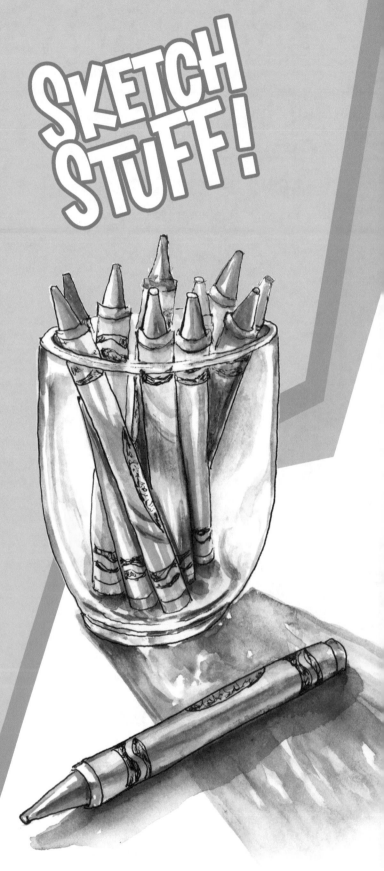

REIMAGINE A CLASSIC STORY!

Creativity isn't always about coming up with something completely new to the world. Sometimes, we can play with ideas that have come before us, and twist them in new ways to make them feel like something fresh and new. The reason a story becomes a classic is that it has something that resonates on a universal level. It touches our hearts and minds.

Think about your favorite book of all time and then reimagine what that story would become if you were the one charged with telling it!

LOST & FOUND

One of the things I do quite often in my sketches is depict animals behaving like humans. I'm also very intrigued by what animals must think about our species and what we abandon and leave behind. Look through an old box of items that you've stored away, while pretending you're an animal discovering them for the first time. What thoughts and ideas come to your mind?

SPEND EACH DAY SKETCHING STUFF!

Now that we've played, explored, and discovered new ideas, it's time to keep going. I hope you've learned that a sketchbook is a playground of thoughts, and that visiting that playground daily will improve your ideas. Whether you write, scribble, or draw, there's a world of new concepts to explore at every moment. Those blank pages can be filled with any thoughts at all, and nothing has to be finished or perfected there. Sketching Stuff is just a way to get ideas flowing so that we can discover our own passions, goals, and fears.

It's a way to abandon our preconceived notions and take the time to explore new paths and possibilities, whether it's in our writing, art, or that next PowerPoint presentation. Everything we do is made better when we use our creativity to approach it.

And, even the most mundane tasks can be made more exciting and engaging when we look at them with fresh eyes. Unlocking something so primal and natural inside each of us seems like it would be super easy.

Yet, this type of thinking and approach to life takes a commitment to practice each and every day. Thankfully, this type of practice is just about playing and having a lot of fun!

If you make it a priority to take even a few precious minutes out of each day to explore ideas in your sketchbook, your life will be much more joyful and exciting. You'll soon discover powers you didn't know you had, and you'll be able to create everything you've ever dreamed.

We all still have that little child inside, imagining the grandest and wildest ideas. Reconnecting with that spirit is as simple as turning to that next beautiful, blank page.

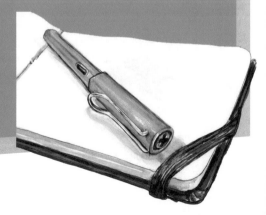

Sketching Stuff™

THANK YOU!
This book was made with love and with the help of people who love me. I couldn't have done it without my husband Philippe who always supports me through all of my zany new ideas. And, a very special thanks to my dear friend Amy Kerr, who helped me catch a million errors (any remaining ones are purely my fault!) and who always pushes me to be a better writer.

Sketching Stuff™

Sketching Stuff™
sketchingstuff.com

From The Creator Of:
doodlewash®
doodlewash.com

THIS IS JUST THE BEGINNING!

We've reached the end of this book, but like all good stories, it's really only the beginning.

Now, it's time to put your creativity to work in everything you do, each and every day. Not only will you come up with bigger and brighter ideas, life itself will become more interesting and fun!

Creativity is one of the most powerful tools we have as human beings. And it's a natural ability that we've had all of our lives. Whether we choose to embrace that ability and harness its power is up to us.

And, if we can tap into the powerful notions and incredible dreams of our Inner Child, we'll be able to make amazing ideas come to life. It's possible to make the seemingly impossible a reality. And it all starts by simply Sketching Stuff!

> " I had the power all along to come home. And home, in this case, was simply going back to the beginning, when I was a child. "

Charlie O.

MEET CHARLIE O.

Well, you've probably figured out by now that I'm basically a big kid who still loves creating new things and coming up with new ideas each and every day. I live in Kansas City, Missouri with my very creative husband who is originally from Paris, France. I love to write and illustrate books, while thinking up all sorts of other wild and zany projects to try next. I'm also the creator of Doodlewash® and founder of World Watercolor Month in July.

Though I continue to dream new dreams, my passion has always remained the same – to inspire people of all ages to create more! We are each beautiful and unique individuals with a special story to tell.

No matter what medium you use, I hope that you'll tell your story through all of the wonderful ideas that you create next.

Please join me via my website below and send me a note. I'd love to hear from you!